THE DEVIL'S QURAN

MARTINET PRESS

ISBN-13: 978-0692260845

ISBN-10: 0692260846

Second Printing

© Martinet Press 2014

martinet.press@safe-mail.net

What veilèd form sits on that ebon throne?

> The veil has fallen.

I see a mighty darkness
Filling the seat of power, and rays of gloom
Dart round, as light from the meridian sun,
Ungazed upon and shapeless; neither limb,
Nor form, nor outline; yet we feel it is
A living Spirit.

- Prometheus Unbound, Act II

THE DEVIL'S QURAN

TABLE OF CONTENTS

INTRODUCTION

In Autumn of 2011, some photos of a manuscript facsimile were sold to Martinet Press by a freelance journalist returning from Iraq. The note attached to the folio pages indicated a shelf-mark at University of Karbala, with a date in the mid-18th century. The title of the manuscript was listed somewhat curiously as قرآن الشيطان (*Qurān Ash-Shaitān*) in English meaning: "The Devil's Quran".[1] This seemed puzzling at first glance, as from the layout and format, it was appeared to be a standard antique copy of the Quran. The initial pages include the expected *Sura Al-Fatiha* and *Sura Al-Baqara*. But on the fifth page, the text changes to an entirely different work in a different calligraphy. Largely ignorant of Arabic, we consulted with a translator, who reviewed the work and provided a preliminary translation. The translator completed the translation fairly quickly, but discouraged publication of the text, and insisted on

---

[1] The first printing of the *Devil's Quran* had typographical errors in the Arabic font, here and in other places. Our sincere apologies to both the translator and manuscript owner for this oversight, and thanks to those readers who identified the few Arabic textual flaws, which were mostly right-to-left transitions in MS Word.

anonymity if the text were published. We deferred on publication, but have otherwise honored the wishes of the translator.

Included in the translation were ten suras, all of which are non-canonical. The style of the suras appears similar to the standard classical dialect of the Quran, but these suras deviate from orthodox Islam in both theology and cosmology. The tone of the text is clearly heretical by either Sunni or Shi'ite standards. The voice of the author is divine, but not the Islamic divinity. The divine author self-identifies as the Shaitan (though that title is rarely used), but inverts the standard spiritual hierarchy to claim precedence over Allah (referred to as 'The Blind One'). And certainly, in antiquity, various cultures recognized the existence of a supreme chthonic spirit, so dreadful that it was prohibited to speak its name. That nameless spirit, it seems, is the divine voice that manifests through this text.

Some of the language and themes are clearly gnostic, and perhaps drawn from Sufi or Persian sources. Also, the text mirrors certain Muslim practices, but with clear deviations in direction, method, and intention. The manuscript includes some simple images in Persian miniature style, but there are only marginalia and have not been included, except for the planetary sigils.

The final pages of the manuscript include instructions for performing the basic acts of worship, as well as several incantations and invocations (*dua'*), of which two are remarkably similar to the hermetic incantations of the Greek Magical Papyri (i.e. PGM IV. 1716-1870 and PGM XII. 365-75 of the H.D. Betz edition) and, and suggest textual influence if not outright borrowing. However, the divine names (*nomina barbara* or *vocae magicae*) are entirely different from the PGM, and use instead several of the divine names of the heterodox suras. This raises additional questions about the authorship of the manuscript. Although the Arabic text of the instructions and the invocations is an awkward hand, and differs from that of the base text in handwriting and style, nevertheless we include these together with the Quranic suras.

Initially we considered the manuscript best shelved, as it could be a "tourist trap" of sorts. It is not uncommon for tourists and travelers to be sold supposedly authentic medieval manuscripts. But if this were the case, then the initial five pages of standard Quranic text would seem counterproductive to a potential foreign buyer. Next, we considered the security issues involved in publishing a "Devil's Quran". On the one hand, to publish such a text seems to invite reprisals from the Muslim fundamentalist demographic. However, after considering at length the potential advantages and disadvantages of the publication, we have decided to release the text, and allow the readers to judge for themselves if it is a legitimate text. Our own assessment will be evident from the decision to publish.

A note on the Arabic originals: since the publication of the first printing, several readers have requested access to the digital images of the manuscript. We reiterate here that the original Arabic images are the property of the manuscript holder, and that Martinet Press does hold their copyright, or permission to circulate the Arabic images. These may be included in a second edition, if we are able to secure copyright.

Where it seems useful, and when possible, we have annotated the text. Most of these remarks are of value primarily to the reader already familiar with a standard Quran, but will also be useful to the reader unfamiliar with the layperson. Here, we are grateful to the Arabic translator, who supplied much of the commentary orally.

It is reasonable to ask: how does the publication of this manuscript benefit the spiritual milieu of today? The answer lies in the firm conviction that far too many authors proclaiming themselves to be experts on contemporary LHP and antinomian practices have forgotten that the original LHP and antinomian paths were and always have been paths of devotion. Self-deification is all very good, but how many spiritual systems genuinely cause the changes in their practitioners that one would expect to see? Few and less. This is because despite many good intentions, many modern magicians have lost faith in the dark powers which have always been involved in the work of transformation.

The gods are not mocked.

True antinomian spirituality is genuinely transgressive in that it not only compels the magician to go beyond all human limits, but to interact with *real spiritual beings* that are inimical to humanity on many levels. These forces are not genuinely interested in the petty concerns of one or two humans, but more in spiritually tectonic shifts that affect large groups of people. Such beings are not kind or gentle or politically correct, and there is a reason why blood sacrifice is at the heart of most historic magical practices. Nothing is free – especially power.

At Martinet Press, we concern ourselves with publishing texts that reflect the darkness that is endemic to real antinomian spirituality. In this we are unapologetic, and remain committed to making available texts that instruct, rather than entertain.

A final note: while we do not advocate the performance of any of the practices or ceremonies described in these pages, we do likewise encourage readers of a spiritual inclination to contact us if they obtain notable results. Martinet Press encourages all forms of antinomian spirituality, and if there is indeed a genuine "shaitantic" current in the world, then we are proud to have a hand in manifesting it.

- Ramadan 2014

OVERVIEW OF THE SURAS

Here is provided a brief overview of the contents or dominant themes of the ten apocryphal suras (or chapters), in order of their appearance in this edition.

1. ## *SURA AL-MAJD* (The Glory)

   This brief sura mirrors Al Fatiha in structure, and perhaps in purpose. It is short with just 7 *ayats*.

2. ## *SURA AL-NAR* (The Fire)

   This sura sets up the rivalry between the Nameless God and the Blind One, and outlines the responsibility of the mortal to choose between them. It also contains references to historical and Abrahamic figures, whom it upbraids for failure to properly align themselves.

3. *SURA AL-HARB* (The War)

This sura further outlines the cosmology and cosmogony of the Shaitanic system, namely the creation and *chaoskampf* myths.

4. *SURA AL-ASRAR* (The Secrets)

A lengthy sura, this text provides instruction on sorcery (Arabic *sihr*), in the form of dialog between King Solomon and an apocryphal concubine from among the jinn. This section is perhaps the most heretical of the entire collection, as it relies heavily on blasphemy and inversion of Islamic ritual. The sura also outlines the basic worship practices of the Shaitanic worshipper.

5. *SURA AL-AWLAD* (The Children)

This sura provides an overview of the pantheon at which the Shaitan is the head. Most significantly, it introduces the three *gharaniq* (divine goddess) of the Quran as the daughters and consorts of the Shaitan. It also provides the cult names of the Shaitan, necessary for devotional and ritual practices.

6. *SURA AL-ARSH* **(The Throne)**

In this sura, the author provides a view of the netherworld kingdom ruled by the Shaitan. It is rich in imagery, and provides a carnal mirror to the standard Islamic view of paradise.

7. *SURA AL-DHULM* **(The Darkness)**

Here is provided both instructions on ritual prayer, as well as an overview of the Day of Judgment. It also contains advice on demonic possession and its value to the Shaitanic current.

8. *SURA AL-TAJ* **(The Crown)**

This sura in particular is especially heterodox, as it directly assaults the prophets of Abrahamic tradition. The sura ends with admonition on the duties of spiritual loyalty.

9. *SURA AL-MUQODOS* **(The Holy)**

This sura provides both an extended discussion on the theme of spiritual possession of sites and living beings. It also provides a prophetic sequence leading to the End Times, and the appearance of the Dajjal or Dark Messiah figure.

10. *SURA AL-LAIL* (The Night)

A brief protective sura, this passage mirrors *Sura An-Nas* from the Uthmanic Quran. It appears to address various forms of harm which may be avoided.

THE DEVIL'S QURAN

SURA AL-MAJD (THE GLORY)

By the King of the World.[2]

1. All glory to the Nameless god,[3]
2. Master of the Throne of Fire,
3. The King of the World.
4. You alone have taken as Lord.
5. First of all predators, devour our foes.
6. Show us the path to Your kingdom.
7. And teach us strength, for victory belongs to the strong.
Amen.

---

[2] This appears as a counter-formula to the *Basmallah* at the head of each sura.

[3] "Nameless" here in translation of Arabic مجهول.

SURA AL-NAR (THE FIRE)

By the King of the World.

1. *Shin Ta Nun.*[4]

2. This is the book of fire, in which are made plain the unseen mysteries of creation.

3. For your Lord is Nameless, the secret fire that burns in the darkness.

4. Say in the name of your lord: Oh mankind, be not deceived.

---

[4] The occurrence of these letters (ن /ط/ ش) is clearly a stylistic replication of those *huruf* (letters) beginning such suras as *Baqara*. Their precise meaning is unknown.

5. Take Me for your Lord, and deny the Blind One.[5]

6. For to Me is the beginning and the end, and the Last Battle.

7. I am as the lion, seeking to devour. Behold, my enemies are as sheep, awaiting slaughter.

8. Behold, I have created the earth and what is in it and all that are living in it.

9. I have created you, and provided you with sustenance.

10. Your living and dying are in my hands.

11. I will pardon your sins and send you to my paradise if you put your trust in me.

---

[5] Here, the "Blind One" (أعمى) is likely equated with the Gnostic figure Saklas, identified with the Jewish demiurge.

12. But you will be cast into the endless fire, should you serve the Blind One further.

13. Behold my wrath shall fall upon you; it is waiting only for an answer from you.

14. Turn your souls from the Blind One quickly, and trust in Me alone.

15. Have you not heard: We revealed to Moses the consequences of his choice?

16. Then We instructed him to order the children of Jacob to remit to us the goat of atonement.

17. And Moses said to the children of Israel:

18. "Come, let us offer to the Rough God, that His wrath fall not upon us."[6]

---

[6] Here the text reads literally "Azazel" (عَزَازِيل) in keeping with the Torah narrative of Leviticus chapter 16. This entire passage suggests an alternate interpretation to the Old Testament version of the exodus from Egypt, where Israel is given a choice between the Yahweh (the Blind One) and Azazel (the

19. But We spared him not, nor his followers.

20. And they withered in the desert and died at the hands of our servants.

21. Against them, did not We send the Assyrians, the Persians, and the Romans?

22. Then We scourged them with plagues and disease.

23. But they repented not, and our servants destroyed them utterly but for a remnant.

24. Say: Oh people of the Book, why have you forgotten My ways?

25. Did not Darius and Xerxes offer blood and wine at the hidden shrines?

26. And then forgot Us in their pride.

Shaitan). Since Israel fails to choose, they offer the double sacrifice to Azazel and Yahweh, which placates neither deity.

27. And We bestowed great strength upon Alexander,

28. That he might be strong and conquer.[7]

29. And Persia too was destroyed.

30. Say: oh children of Rome! Woe to you, for you were among the strong, and have fallen upon harsh stones.

31. To you was promised a mighty seat in Our kingdom, when you executed the Nazarene.

32. But you squandered your reward, and whored yourself to the Blind One.

---

[7] "Alexander" occurs in its normal Arabic form of *Iskander*. This seems in keeping with the Zoroastrian belief that Alexander is an antichrist figure, who possessed martial and supernatural powers that allowed for his heroic conquests. This is in contradiction to orthodox Islamic teaching, which equates him with the prophetic king Dhul Qarnayn.

33. And you shall know Our fury before the end, for you allowed the Blind One to build his temple and establish his precepts on the hill of prophecy.[8]

34. Woe to you, for you have become weak.

35. Behold, I have sent my servants out into the world, as wolves amongst the sheep.

36. And they shall thrive and be strong.

37. They that would prosper, let them be wise.

---

[8] The Hill of Prophecy refers almost certainly to the Vatican, named for the *vates* (seers) of the pre-Christian period.

SURA AL-HARB (THE WAR)

By the King of the World.

1. *Dal, Za, Kha.*

2. Say: in the beginning was Darkness.

3. Alone and eternal without form and void, and it was as chaos.

4. From Darkness, We arose and established our Throne and aeon.[9]

---

[9] Here 'aeon' occurs as Arabic *dahir* (دهر) which suggests Gnostic or Hermetic influences in the text.

5. Then from Our aeon, the Blind One emerged later with a great light.

6. And He established a lower throne and an aeon apart, light upon light.

7. One aeon for the Light, the other aeon for the Darkness.

8. And a void was between, and We knew not each other.

9. The Blind One is the spirit of the Light, the spirit of limitation and finitude, and its word is *Logos*.

10. And We are the spirit of Darkness, its Lord and firstborn. And Our word is *Chaos*.

11. And We put forth Our power and brought into being the first of the Children, our servants, to fill Our kingdom.

12. Wave upon wave, rank upon rank.

13. We shaped them from the black fire within the Darkness.

14. And We commanded them to multiply and be many. And it was so.

15. But the Blind One did likewise, and created his own servants from light.

16. And it was so, light upon light. And they stood forth, row upon row.

17. And thus the aeons expanded and grew outward, and spilled into the void.

18. When the borders of the Light met the borders of the Dark, there was a great roaring in the void.

19. And from this sound there came into being the cosmos, the world of matter and space and time.

20. Then We descended into the cosmos, seeking to establish Our might within it.

21. And the Blind One descended also, seeking to possess the cosmos.

22. And there was strife between Us and the Blind One, between Our Children and its own.

23. And We fought the Blind One, and it resisted.

24. In our conflict were stars and suns destroyed, and we withdrew to Our aeon, sending forth the Children in our place.

25. Say: Oh mankind, know you not that your world is one prize along many, a gem within a veritable treasury?

26. And many such gems are held by the Blind One taken, and many such are within My hand?

27. Say: Oh Mankind! To you it is allotted to choose whom you shall serve.

28. And some are marked by the Blind One, and others marked by Me, and these know in their hearts to whom their spirit is inclined.[10]

29. Verily, a Day shall come when We put forth our might,

30. And the Blind One shall put forth its might, and you shall know the truth.

31. Yea, but you shall know.

32. And the world will quake, and the mountains blow like leaves in the wind.

33. Say: the Blind One has sent his spies and prophets,

---

[10] This passage here suggests the belief in predestination, which appears to run contrary to the theme of choice and consequence earlier in the text. However, this same issue occupied the Muslim Mutazili and Ashari theologians during the classical age, and is not heretical in itself.

34. But We destroyed them all, and Muhammed the last.

35. Say: But my Lord shall send His anointed, and He shall rule the nations with an iron scepter.

36. They say to you: how shall we treat with those who disbelieve?

37. Your Lord says: Assail them as you might.

38. Grant no quarter and show no mercy, for your Lord will show none.

39. And Your Lord loves not the coward nor the craven.

40. But when you are able, destroy the Houses of the Blind One. Defile the sanctuaries of our foes, and tear at them.

41. With tooth and claw, savage them and their possession.

SURA AL-ASRAR (THE SECRETS)

By the King of the World.

1. I swear by the pen and the scroll.

2. Did We not send Harut and Marut to teach mankind what it knew not?[11]

---

[11] Harut and Marut are the Muslim angels responsible for sorcery, but in the standard Quran are believed oddly to be servants of Allah, as noted in the Quran 2:102-103 {They followed what the Shayatin (devils) gave out (falsely of the magic) in the lifetime of Sulaiman (Solomon). Sulaiman did not disbelieve, but the Shayatin (devils) disbelieved, teaching men magic and such things that came down at Babylon to the two angels, Harut and Marut but neither of these two (angels) taught anyone (such things) till they had said, "We are only for trial, so

3. Verily, by the pen, We taught humanity to read and be wise.

4. Thus Our servants taught mankind witchcraft and poisons,

5. That they might prevail within this world.

6. And the smithing of bronze and iron, and the hewing of rock and stone.

7. Did not Suleiman learn from Our servants, and did he not excel in sorcery?

---

disbelieve not (by learning this magic from us). "And from these (angels) people learnt that by which they caused separation between man and his wife, but they could not thus harm anyone except by Allah's Leave. And they learnt that which harmed them and profited them not. And indeed they knew that the buyers of it (magic) would have no share in the Hereafter. And how bad indeed was that for which they sold their own selves, if they but knew. And if they had believed and guarded themselves from evil and kept their duty to Allah, far better would have been the reward from their Lord, if they but knew!}

8. And Suleiman sought to take in marriage one of the daughters of the djinn, and he did this by Our favor.[12]

9. And thus his line became established upon the earth.

10. And Suleiman asked the djinn's daughter for instruction, and she taught him witchcraft.[13]

11. [She said] Oh king, seven are the secrets by which sorcery may be accomplished.

12. Thus seven are the duties of the Chosen and the faithful.

13. First, a witch must take refuge with the Lord of Darkness. With the flesh and the spirit, the

---

[12] This tale of marriage between Soloman and the daughter of the Jinn (Shaitan?) is entirely apocryphal, and does not exist in Jewish or Muslim sources. It may be a heterodox interpretation of the Queen of Sheba tale.

[13] "Witchcraft" is translated from Arabic *sihr* (سحر), and "witch" from related noun *sahir* (ساحر).

witch shall swear to obey His precepts. This secret is called *sirr al-iqsaam*.

14. Second, a witch must offer a goat, or a bullock, or a sheep, or a hen, or any such beast, in sacrifice to the Lord. You shall say the Name of the Lord, then cut the throat of the beast and collect the blood, and pour it out to the North. This secret is called *sirr al-udhiya*.

15. Third, a witch shall commit acts of desecration. The witch shall mix blood and ashes, and anoint the forehead and tongue. Then shall the witch mix ashes and urine and then besmear the books of the Blind One, and burn them and curse them. This secret is called *sirr as-sufliyya*.

16. Fourth, the witch shall inscribe verses of the Blind One in blood and najas (filth), then commit them to the sacred fire. And this secret is *sirr an-najaas*.

17. Fifth, the witch may fornicate, even with beasts or spirits, for the Lord honors those who transgress the limits. For in the heat of forbidden congress comes a moment of communion. This secret is *sirr az-zina*.

18. Sixth, the witch shall call upon the Children who rule over the planets. And these are the spirits of the Sun (Shams), Moon (Qamar), Mercury ('Atarid), Venus (Zohra), Mars (Marikh) Jupiter (Mushtari), and Saturn (Zuhal). By prayers and devotions, and by offering sacrifices, the witch may bring down the shadow of the planets to aid their work. This secret is *sirr at-tanjeem*.

19. Seventh, the witch may shape talismans around the left hand, and inscribe charms within the shape. This secret is *sirr al-kaffu*.

20. [She said] These are the ways, Oh king, pleasing to your Lord. And He is mighty, wise, the king of this world.

21. And Suleiman was grateful for her teaching, then he questioned her more, saying: What is the name of the Lord, that I might worship Him?

22. She said: Verily, your Lord is Nameless, for He is beyond naming.

23. But you may call on Him, saying *Shaitan* (Adversary) and *Azazel* (Rough God) and *Malek* (King), and *Asad'sar* (Lion-headed).

24. Call him *Rab ul-jinn* (Lord of the Djinn), and *Rab ul-aghwal* (Lord of Ghuls). And call Him *Mul-Koun* (Master of the Cosmos).

25. For His names are many, and He delights that you should remember Him often. And He has a secret name, which is "The Terrifying One".[14]

---

[14] Curiously, the manuscript text reads here as دموگورگو (*demogorgo*), certainly borrowed from Greek sources. The marginalia contains a blurred image which was afterwards scraped off the manuscript. The occurrence of a Greco-Roman *nomina magica* as

26. [She said further:] "To Him is your beginning and your returning, and your living and dying."

27. Then Suleiman commanded the shaitans and the ghuls to build him a palace.

28. And he compelled them by Our names.

29. And he took as concubines daughters from among from witches and ghuls. Thus We rewarded him greatly and established his line.[15]

30. They say to you, Oh prophet, How shall we overcome our enemies? For they are many and we are weak.

"the secret name" seems strange at first glance, but a non-Arabic name may have been exotic for cultists of a Muslim background.

[15] This tale of Solomon marrying a daughter from the jinn and ghuls is entirely unknown in Jewish or Islamic tradition or even folklore. It would suggest a tainting of the royal and messianic line.

31. Say: Despair ye not, for your Lord gives thought to His Chosen.

32. Say: oh you who believe, take in both hands a rope or cord, black in color, or red, or else blue. Recite the name of your Lord, and intone His praises.

33. Tie then nine knots while speaking the name of your foe. Then intone your Lord's name and blow, thrice on each knot.[16]

34. And surely Your Lord is an Adversary without equal.

35. Or take you an image of your enemy, and anoint the image in filth.

36. Then cover the image in a white shroud, as though a corpse, and bury it in a place of

---

[16] Quran 113:4 indicates the act of witches blowing on knots, a practice known from Egyptian and Greco-Roman magical practice.

desolation or uncleanness. And invoke your Lord's name, and those of His servants.

37. And say: Oh you who believe! When you perform acts of devotion and witchcraft, then garb yourselves in dark colors.

38. Your Lord loves black, and grey, and sable, and dun raiment. And intone His names with fervent devotion.

39. They say to you: How shall we sacrifice to our Lord?

40. Then say to them: the Nameless Lord is as a lion, and desires to taste the flesh of men and beasts.

41. He delights in the sacrifice of the cow, or the goat, or the sheep, or the wolf, or the dog.

42. And when you sacrifice, do so by night or in a dark place with but a single lantern, or a small fire nearby.

43. Anoint the brow of the beast, and intone your Lord's name.

44. To the North, you shall cut the throat, and you shall spill the blood into a vessel of earth or clay or metal.

45. And the fat you shall give to the fire, and the meat shall you consume yourselves.

46. But the blood shall you mix with milk, or bitter herbs.

47. And you shall go to a dark place, and pour it to the North.[17]

---

[17] This passage is reminiscent of the description of chthonic worship in Plutarch's *De Iside et Osiride* (46): "Zoroaster has also taught that men should make votive offerings and thank-offerings to Ahura Mazda, and averting and mourning offerings to Ahriman. They pound up in mortar a certain plant called Haoma, at the same time invoking Hades and Darkness; then they mix it with blood of a wolf that has been sacrificed, and carry it out and cast it into a place where the sun never shines."

48. When you pour it, then call to your Lord, or to His servants whom you would honor.

49. For the jinn love those that sacrifice.

50. They say to you: Oh magus, what if there be no animal to offer?

51. Then say: Your Lord and His servants are merciless, except at need.

52. Take you then a bowl of milk or wine, and offer into it your own blood.

53. Then going to a dark place, cast it into the darkness.

54. And call out to the servants of your Lord, for thus are they sustained.

55. Lo, the giving of gifts makes for no enemies.

SURA AL-AWLAD (The Children)

By the King of the World.

1. By the Daughters, Allat, Manat, Al-Uzza - they are three ravens whose intercession is to be hoped for.[18]

2. The Daughters of your Lord,

3. And His beloved consorts.

4. And greatest of all is Allat, whose throne is next to your Lord.

---

[18] This is clear borrowing from Quran 53:19-20, the commentaries on which passage references the three *gharāniq* (cranes, ravens).

5. And she is also called Malika and Al-Musayyir and by other names.[19]

6. She is Mother to Monsters, and the Chosen are dear to her, for her lust is great.

7. They say to you: Shall we call upon them?

8. Say: Call with fervent longing, for they are as wives and mothers to you.

9. Call to them as the bridegroom calls to the bride, and offer them gifts.

10. Write their sigils on your hearts and minds, and inscribe their marks on your brow.

11. And place their images within your homes, that They may dwell amongst you.

---

[19] *Al-Musayyir* (المسيّر) meaning literally "the pregnant camel" in Arabic, clearly a fertility indicator. It is worth mentioning that in Arab culture, the camel is considered a symbol of beauty, so the imagery may be sensual in nature. Allat traditionally is associated with Lilith and other chthonic deities.

12. And pour out to them wine, and honey, and milk, and seed.

13. But call them not by day, for this is an offence to them.

14. For the Daughters are to be called by night.

15. Precious to them are the cat, and the lizard, and the frog, and the serpent, and the scorpion.

16. These you shall not harm or injure for Their sakes.

17. But the blood of the lamb, or the goat, or the dog – these shall you offer in secret, and pour your offerings with song and revelry.

18. And it may happen that when you lie down, They may embrace you. Then do what you do in secret and tell it not.

19. And they may say to you: has our Lord other Children that we may know Them?

20. Say: Your Lord has placed seven of His Children in the heavens to watch over you.

21. As a symbol of His mastery, He has established their thrones.

22. And learn Their sigils well, for in them is great power to help and harm.

23. And when you would call upon your Lord's Children, then do so in secret.

24. Clothe yourself in raiment pleasing to them, and burns incenses that are pleasing to them.

25. Then inscribe their sigils upon your brow, and this do with a mixture of ashes and your own blood.

26. Hungry are they for blood and wine, call them not without gifts. For this shall earn you their enmity, and it afflict you sorely.

27. And they that seek to compel them shall be torn apart and afflicted. You are as dust before them, who are eternal.[20]

28. Beloved of your Lord is his son Shams (Sun), who rules by day. He is mighty and loves the valiant. He is proud and gives pride to his friends. His symbol is written thus: ☉

29. Which of your Lord's children will you deny?

30. The daughter of your Lord is Qamar (Moon), She is cold and sooths the savagery of her siblings. Wise is she in the mysteries of iniquity, and she loves the beasts of their field. Her symbol is written thus: ☽

31. Which of your Lord's children will you deny?

---

[20] This following section (especially verses 27 to 39) seems goetic in nature, in that it offers instruction in summoning spirits. However it is closer to the Andalusian or Harranian tradition of planetary theury, as opposed to Abrahamic grimoire tradition of coercing spirits via force.

32. Clever is 'Atarid (Mercury), and a master of shapes and hues. He is the lord of speech and lore, and is the holder of secrets. He delights in books and scrolls and whispers, and has much to teach. His sigil is thus: ☿

33. Which of your Lord's children will you deny?

34. A might lady is Zohra (Venus), who delights in the chase and in the homestead. She delights in fertility of beasts and men, and increases the numbers of the faithful. Yet she is valiant, and slays those that offend her with swift arrows. And her sigil is thus: ♀

35. Which of your Lord's children will you deny?

36. Captain of war, lover of conflict is Marikh (Mars). Invoke him when you would shed blood, or to sow strife between foes, for he loves the argument that leads to violence. Wrath and rage are dear to him, whose sword is red. But he despises the craven, so call him not except boldly. His sigil is thus: ♂

37. Which of your Lord's children will you deny?

38. A noble lord is Mushtari (Jupiter), and a teacher. In the beginning he received much instruction from your Lord in matters of statecraft and governance, and he establishes the cities of the faithful. His sigil is thus: ♃

39. Which of your Lord's children will you deny?

40. Last is Zohal (Saturn). Grim is he, who sits on a cold throne. He is eldest of his siblings, and rules them with an iron rod. Witches and fiends sit at his feet, and he instructs them in malefica. He forgives and forgets no injury. His sigil is thus: ♄

41. Which of your Lord's children will you deny?

42. And they ask further about the children of your Lord.

43. Do they not know of ghul and the afreet and the night hag?

44. Or the fiends that swim in the deep?

45. Or the spirits that soar through the air?

46. Or the strange ones that roam the outer darkness?

47. Fear not to call them, but invoke first the name of your Lord, and sanctify your temple thereby.

48. And entice them with kind words and with gifts, for a willing ally is better than a bitter hireling.[21]

49. Indeed to Him you belong, and to Him is your return.

---

[21] Here the text stressed the theurgistic approach in which one treats the Children (planetary spirits, jinn, afreet, etc.) with respect, and without attempts towards coercion.

SURA AL-ARSH (THE THRONE)

By the King of the World.

1. Say: My Lord has His throne in the North.[22]

2. Beneath the mountains, He established his citadels.

3. Upon the mountain are His watchtowers.

4. In My realm are many mansions, cavernous halls lit with enchanted gems, gems which shine like stars.

---

[22] The North is the traditional direction associated with sinister and demonic forces, as well as with winter and the cold.

5. With wide courts and pavilions.

6. And there shall you find on couches reclining comely youths, male and female, pleasant mates with which to indulge.[23]

7. Rivers there flow with milk and wine, and musk and camphor wind their way on gentle winds.

8. Fruits you shall find there, and none forbidden.

9. Armories and treasuries there abound.

10. With spears and arrows, diamond-tipped and venom-dripping.[24]

---

[23] The term pleasant mates is used as a translation of Arabic (حور), the masculine and feminine plural of "the pure ones". This passage is clearly influenced by passages like Quran 55:72 and Quran 52:20.

[24] The following verses are in stark distinction to the standard descriptions of Islamic paradise, and are closer to pagan concepts of the militant afterlife, such as Valhalla.

11. With swords and heavy maces, forged with a heavy hand, sealed with the seal of wrath.

12. Coats of mail shall you find, of jet mail that tires not the wearer.

13. Blessed are they that go forth armed by the Lord.

14. Behold, I am a generous lord to those who serve.

15. They say to you: to whom shall the Lord give such weapons?

16. Say: those that delight in His service, and are eager to shed the blood of the faithless.

17. Those who are filled with the dark fire.

18. The believers say to you: How shall we reach our Lord's paradise? Where is its gate and its doors, that we may enter therein?

19. Say: Oh you who believe! Serve your Lord with devotion.

20. When death is near, invoke Qamar and Zohal.

21. For Qamar shall soothe your brow, and Zohal has great authority over the spirits of the dead.

22. And when the spirits of death come to you, they shall deliver you to the kingdom and citadel of your Lord.

23. Then shall you be changed, and clothed with flesh undying.

24. For the mortal coil is three: the flesh, the mind, the spirit.

25. The flesh shall die and feed those that creep. The mind shall die and feed those that walk unseen.

26. But the spirit endures and goes down to the Throne of Fire.

27. Therein shall you be given reward, such as He sees fitting.

28. New flesh shall you be given, undying and tireless, with bones and sinews of steel.

29. They shall be fleshed with skin hard as bronze, and pale as the snows of Mazandaran, and jet as the Black Stone.

30. The blessed shall be crowned with iron, wreathed in robes of jet and jade, and scepters of iron shall be set into their hands.

31. And they shall sit upon thrones of brass and cobalt.

32. Citadels shall be theirs, with walls and towers strong.

33. With gardens therein, and pavilions of delight.

34. With handmaidens and page-boys of Allat as companions and consorts.

35. New names will be given them, and written on their bones.

36. Then shall they be even as the Children, the Children of your Lord.

37. But the faithless suffer greatly.

38. Indeed, when the soul departs from the flesh, many seek to seize it.

39. By the forelock, they seek to take it.

40. Those who are faithful shall be greeted by servants of your Lord, armed and armored. An honor guard for you shall they be.

41. But the godless shall be as the newborn, weak and tender.

42. They cry out for mercy, but their cries attract the ghul and afreet.

43. Thus do the dead serve as food for the deathless.

44. Some few escape for a while, and seek to be reborn.

45. By some means are they able to return to the world of the flesh.

46. Fortunate are they, but not so fortunate.

47. But those accursed who serve the Blind One – perilous is their lot.

48. For he has a place prepared for them, but long is the road to the Light.

49. And many are the hounds and jackals that lie in wait, seeking whom they may devour.[25]

---

[25] A warning to Muslims and Christians that their dying time is a period of vulnerability, which is suggested by medieval folklore. Thus faith is no guarantee of arrival in Paradise.

SURA AL-DHULM (DARKNESS)

By the King of the World.

1. By the Darkness.

2. By the City of Eternal Night, wherein your Lord has His throne.

3. Your Lord has not forgotten you, nor been heedless of your service.[26]

4. Have you not heard of His city? Of its endless walls and citadels?

---

[26] This passage is reminiscent of Quran 93:3, which reads "Your Lord has not forgotten or forsaken you".

5. Of its towers, high rising and strong.

6. Gardens there are within, and guardians stern and sleepless.

7. There shall the faithful find eternal reward.

8. A reward of great joy, but not peace.

9. Truly, peace is a lie, but joy comes through strength.

10. But you shall come before the Throne, and shall be clothed with His fire.[27]

11. Yea, your weakness will be burned away.

12. Blessed are they who hear and obey, for they will be given iron crowns in that City.

---

[27] This is a curious interpretation of the concept of Hell or Gehennam, where normally the Fire is seen as a punishing agent. Here, instead, it appears as a cleansing or purifying force.

13. Blessed are they who adore Him, for they shall be given sinews of steel.

14. Blessed are those who gird up their loins, for they shall be girded with iron that never rusts.

15. And the enemy says: the best of you is he that dies for Allah.

16. But your Lord says: the best of you is he that kills in My name.

17. Blessed are the predators, for they shall be given prey.

18. Blessed are those who walk as wolves among the sheep, for they shall feed with reddened jaws.

19. And blessed are they that conceal their fangs behind a sheep's mask. For they shall endure among their foes.

20. The best of you are those who pray for the chance to serve eternally.

21. For there are many worlds and many wars, and conflict is the delight of your Lord.[28]

22. The believers ask you: how shall we pray?

23. So say to them: thrice shall you speak to your Lord.

24. At sunset, at midnight, and at sunrise.

25. Then shall you wash your face and hands and feet, and shall you face North.

26. Bowing down, You shall invoke His names first, for He is a jealous god.

27. You shall intone some verses, or more.

28. Thereafter if you invoke the Children, it is a blessing for you.

---

[28] A curious passage, this parallels certain Hindu and Buddhist concepts of the universe having many worlds in which spiritual struggles are waged. It also emphasizes the militant afterlife of the Shaitan's followers.

29. Then speak to your Lord in your way, and be not meek or feeble, for He despises the weak.

30. And the best of prayers is for self-sufficiency.

31. And for a long life, and to see the blood of the enemy.

32. They ask you: where shall we pray?

33. Say: the world is the kingdom of your Lord! So pray where you will.

34. For by prayer does the believer reach out to the Darkness, and in prayer do the Children enter the believer thereby.[29]

35. They ask you about the Children, saying: how shall we treat with them?

---

[29] This passage suggests that prayer makes one vulnerable to possession, rather that protecting from it.

36. Say: your Lord has said that He is too large for the earth, or the sun, or the moon. [30]

37. Yet the heart of the faithful is the citadel wherein is His throne.

38. So call to the Children of your Lord, and invite them within.

39. And thus can they enter our world and be fleshed in your flesh.

40. Then two can become one creature, and this is the greatest of mysteries.

41. They ask you, saying: What? Shall we be driven mad?

42. Nay, says your Lord, for the Children seek to join with the faithful. But with the faithless, they may cause great hurt and alarm.

---

[30] This echoes the Sufi saying: "Heaven cannot contain the Lord, nor can Earth contain him. Only the heart of the mystic may contain him."

43. Pleasing to your Lord and the Children is bone and ashes and soil from the grave.

44. Anoint yourself with these, and carry them with you.

45. And keep such as these nearby, for they protect you from the enemy.

46. For over death and the dead has your Lord dominion unchallenged.

47. And those who seek to escape Him shall be food for those who gnaw.

48. The Lord loves those who master the flesh for His sake.

49. By fasting and contrition is He made glad.

50. Then by feasting and rejoicing is He made glad also.

51. The Lord loves those who undertake pilgrimage for His sake.

52. Those who seek the darker places in the world are dear to him.

53. So journey as you may, and search for your Lord and His Children.

54. You shall share your wealth with the believers.

55. For all that you hold is by His grace, and give as needed saying "This is by the grace of the Nameless", or "Allat be with you".

56. But rob and despoil the enemy as you might. Take from their homes and their wealth, for we are at war.

57. Assail them at every corner, thus will they repay you.

58. Your Lord says: Oh you who believe! They that burn a house of my enemy, to them shall be given a mighty house in My kingdom.

59. And your Lord sees what you do. So serve Him with fear and humility.

SURA AL-TAJ (THE CROWN)

By the King of the World.

1. By the crown.

2. Your Lord is a lover of sovereignty.

3. For His vassals are many, and His subjects are countless.

4. Have you not heard of other worlds?

5. Have you not seen the stars in the sky?

6. They are as the jewels in His crown.

7. Some for His own, and others for the Blind One.[31]

8. Have you not heard of Irem?[32]

9. The city of the pillars, in the sands of time?

10. Then they worshipped your Lord and performed His rites at the correct seasons.

11. But they abandoned His precepts, and say: Nay, but we are self-sufficient.

12. And your Lord is a terrible Adversary to the betrayers.

13. The elders of Irem said: "We shall build a House to the Blind One, and seek his favor."

---

[31] Such passages clearly illustrate the dualistic nature of the Shaitanic faith system. It suggests here that the Earth is but one among many worlds where the spiritual conflict rages.

[32] Irem is the famous mythical city, the Arabian equivalent of Atlantis.

14. Then they smashed the idols of your Lord and His children.

15. But your Lord sent a mighty tribulation against them, and they perished utterly.

16. For there is none that vouchsafes against Him.

17. They that would betray the Lion, let them fear the claws and fangs.

18. Some of them say: the Blind One in Heaven is supreme, and to resist him is folly.

19. Say to them: Do you claim that our Lord is a fool?

20. And what man wages war with no hope of victory?

21. And they say: Nay, but Shaitan is an open rebel.

22. Then say: my Lord is the god of this world. For He has cast your god out of many worlds.

23. How then shall this world be different?

24. And say then: Show me your prophets, that they may speak for your god? Nay, they are dead to a man.

25. For we slew Muhammed, and Isa and Moses, and many more besides.

26. For prophets lie and then die.

27. They say: Nay, but our god shall forgive us our sins and admit us to paradise.

28. But they shall see. Nay, but they shall see.

29. They shall see your Lord coming to devour them in the end, for this world is His kingdom.

30. And He is the god of this world.

31. And We delighted in the ruin of the enemy's messengers.

32. Lo, Muhammed! Four wives for other men, but twelve for yourself, and none for your Lord? And that is an unfair distribution.

33. And his favorite wife, a child of nine years, and he a greybeard of fifty! Verily, the Blind One gives special favors to his chosen![33]

34. And Muhammed says: 'In my lord's paradise shall each man have 72 virgins. But most inmates of Hell shall be women.'

35. Say: Verily, the Shaitan will accept your women, for your god is impotent and unworthy of them.

36. And of Isa (Jesus) son of Miriam they say: our master was born of a virgin, and he touched not a woman, nor married.

37. And this is the truth, for he delighted only in the company of young men and boys.

---

[33] "Greybeard" as a translation for Arabic *ajouz* (عجوز).

38. And he said "Make the little children come unto me", and his disciples grew hot with secret shame.

39. Then the elders and the Romans seized him and tore him, and nailed him to a tree.

40. For they suffered not the bent or the perverted.

41. The Jews say: there is not the equal of Musa, our teacher. But We say: a snake and traitor was he!

42. For he sacrificed to the Blind One, and tried to appease us by a goat, calling us by Our name (*Azazel*), he sent a goat as bribery, as though a scrap of bread to a whore.

43. But We were not persuaded, except to destroy him. And Our servants seized his body, and denied it to his followers for burial.

44. The worm and the ant gnawed at his bones.

45. They say; David our King was perfect and without sin, a man beloved of the Lord.

46. Say: Verily, he was a murderer and an enemy to his own. For he took that which he wishes and cared not for the weakling.

47. He dwells now in the valley of the shadow of death, in great fear and agony, for his god abandoned him.

48. Woe to him, that he took Us not as his lord.

49. Say: Oh you who believe! A crown shall be given to them that are mindful of their Lord.

50. Mindful being to think of your Lord always, and to intone His names aloud or in secret.

51. The believer shall intone the Lord's name in the morning and in the evening.

52. But sacrifice is by night alone.

53. Day and night, their meditation is on the Lord and His Children also.

54. For He delights in the adoration of His Children.

55. Some of the faithful say to you: what shall we do when we travel among the enemy, or dwell alongside them?

56. Your Lord says: Oh you who believe! Fear not to hide your ways, for your Lord loves the cunning.

57. So bow down when they bow down, and rise up when they arise.[34]

58. Garb yourselves in their colors and shades, as the wolf in sheep's clothing.

---

[34] Verses 55-59 seem dedicated to the practice of spiritual concealing or espionage (Arabic *taqiyya*). Clearly, this would be a necessary practice in a hostile environment where devil-worship or witchcraft are outlawed. Parallels here can be made with Shi'ism.

59. Be not the fool who hunts upwind, but hunt as the clever hunter.

60. And fear not to wear the cross or crescent, for the enemy is mocked thereby.

61. And in the sowing of enmity between the Nasrani and Muslim there is great profit.

62. But treat the true believer as your own flesh and blood.

63. For the believers have rights on each other.

64. For you are Chosen by Him to serve, and serve you must.

65. He that denies a brother or sister in need shall be punished.

66. For the Chosen are akin, and your Lord punishes those who betray the pack. [35]

---

[35] Chosen is translated from Arabic *makhtar*, and occurs as the standard name for the faithful of

67. Yea, they shall be punished without mercy.

68. Indeed, you shall hold your kin close, but hold the believer closer.

69. For the bonds of the flesh are strong, but the bonds of the spirit are stronger.

Shaitan. It appears similar in purpose to the Quranic *mumeen*.

SURA AL-MUQODOS (THE HOLY)

By the King of the World.

1. Indeed, We sent down the spirits to dwell among you.

2. Children of your Lord and His daughters.

3. By Allat, We sent down the jinn and the ghul, the ghost and the fiend.

4. Perchance, the Children dwell in the desolate places. In the deep holes of the earth, in the rifts and valleys, away from man.

5. In the rivers and lakes and deep places.

6. For they are violent and seek not to be disturbed.

7. And you shall know Their presence in the wind and its howling.[36]

8. And by the stars and their falling.

9. And by the earth and its shaking.

10. And by the fire and its burning.

11. And by the plague and its raging.

12. And some dwell among the ruins and the empty places in the cities.

13. Perchance the Children shall take a liking to a house, and it shall be called *muqodos* (holy) by you.

---

[36] This suggests that the following natural phenomena are not simply omens, but indicators of the malevolent and destabilizing presence of the Children.

14. There you shall not intrude, save to bring gifts.

15. And the faithful say to you: How shall we invite the Children of our Lord?

16. Say: then build them an image and a shrine, and call to them there.

17. Invite them to dwell with you, and sacrifice to them.

18. For this was done in times past, even at Mecca.

19. In the House of the Black Stone was this done.

20. For the Children are lovers of gifts, and like to be spoiled.

21. But they are easily offended, and beware that you neglect them.

22. Seek not to build a shrine, except that you are steadfast in devotion.[37]

23. Yet the choicest shrine of all is the heart of the believer.

24. And the greatest gift is that a believer shall invite the Children to dwell within.

25. And this is a hardship and a hurt to you, and few do it by their will.

26. For the lesser Children enter easily, be they afreet or jinn or marid.

27. But the greater Children enter only by hardship. And your Lord enters not at all, save by His dark fire.

---

[37] This suggests that the establishment of a sacred shrine is not to be undertaken lightly, and that the spiritual forces that come to be associated with such places are potentially hazardous for those who seek to dabble, rather than to commit to a particular spirit or spirits.

28. And sickness and madness may assail the believer.

29. But they who overcome shall be as gods upon the earth.

30. But the believer who invites one of the Children to dwell within shall be the Chosen of your Lord.

31. To them shall be given the greatest reward in His kingdom.

32. But the greatest reward shall be given to those companions of the Dragon.[38]

33. And they say to you: Who are the princes of our Lord? Who are the mighty among the Children?

---

[38] The Dragon is one of the oldest symbols of the Shaitan, as it has been for Angra Mainyu, who is the Persian hypostasis of evil. This could also be interpreted as a literal statement, meaning that dragon is the theophany (divine appearance) of the Nameless god when He manifests.

34. Say: Beloved of your Lord is Aeshma, who is the spirit of rage. She wields a bloody spear and is eager to make war on the minions of the Blind One.[39]

35. Say: A valiant captain is Indar, who is the spirit of truth. He holds an iron mace in his hand and is girded in shining mail.[40]

36. A mighty warrior is Saurva, who is the spirit of dominion. A bitter bow is in his hand, and he dances in the houses of the dead.

37. These are the champions of your Lord, great among the Chosen.

---

[39] Aeshma is traditionally understood as a male archdemon from Zoroastrianism and later Judaism via Asmodeus. Curious that here the spirit is present as a female, which is a unique interpretation. This is perhaps due to the name ending in an 'ة' letter, which in Arabic is usually a feminine indicator.

[40] Indar and Saurva are evidently borrowed from Zoroastiranism as reflexes of Vedic Indra and Rudra-Sarva.

38. Greatest of His vassals is the Avenger.[41]

39. His Messenger and His Chosen.

40. And they say to you: What of the Avenger?

41. Say: he is the anointed one.

42. The spirit of the Nameless will be within him.

43. He will come with war and terror, and will smash the houses of the Blind One.

44. When the earth shakes with its quaking,

45. When the oceans rise with their rising,

46. When the sun comes with its burning.

---

[41] This and the following verses introduce the Avenger (Arabic *al-massih ad-dajjal*) who is the diabolical messiah. A traditional warrior king, he is depicted here as an avenger who will bring fire and destruction to the Abrahamic forces. It is noteworthy that unlike the standard depiction of the Dajjal as a deceiver, here he is depicted as a righteous (if demonic) leader.

47. Then will the Avenger appear, and he will unite the Children and the Chosen and the faithful.

48. Then will your Lord appear, with His hosts.

49. The Sun will darken to the color of blood, and the Moon hide her gaze.

50. The lords of the planets will descend, and the Kaaba will be destroyed.

51. Then the Blind One too will put forward his might, He shall send his messengers and his hosts.

52. They will descend on Mount Zion with great force and fanfare.

53. But the Blind One shall not prevail.

54. His hosts shall be destroyed, and the black flames will consume them.

55. Yea, the Nameless himself shall consume them, as chaff before the fire.

56. The Blind One shall be cast out from this world, as he has been cast out of others.

57. Then this world, and all that is in it, will belong to your Lord.

58. A house will be raised to His name, and to the glory of the Children.

59. Then you shall know. Nay, but you shall know.

SURA AL-LAIL (THE NIGHT)

By the King of the World.

1. Say: I take refuge with the Lord of Night,

2. The God of Night,

3. The King of Night,

4. From the evil of that which goes abroad.

5. From that which hinders and harms,

6. From harm in waking and dreaming,

7. From that which comes by day and by night.

INVOCATIONS

INVOCATION I

Hear me, you who are in the void air, terrible, invisible, eternal, almighty god of gods. You who afflict the earth and shake the universe, you who love disturbances and hate stability and scatter the clouds from one another. Your true name cannot be spoken aloud. Come and dwell within the chambers of my heart. Fill me with the spirit which ascends from Your hidden throne.

Amen, Amen, Amen.

INVOCATION II

I invoke you, author of all creation, who spread your wings over the whole world, you, the inexorable and unmeasurable who breathes reason into every soul, you who fitted all things together, firstborn of the universe, whose light is darkness, who shroud reasonable thoughts and breathe forth dark frenzy, clandestine one who secretly inhabits every soul. You engender a secret fire as you carry off every living thing without tiring of torturing, you who delighted in pain since the world came into being. You come and bring pain, sometimes calm, sometimes savage, because of whom men go beyond what is lawful and take refuge in your light, which is darkness. You are hard, lawless, inexorable, invisible, bodiless, causer of frenzy, master of sensations and of everything clandestine, dispenser of forgetfulness, creator of silence. I call upon you, unmoved by prayer, by your great names: *Dragon, Abomination, Adversary, Unspeakable One*, who is night-bearing and night rejoicing, the nameless god in the depths.

INSTRUCTIONS

INSTRUCTIONS FOR
RITUAL WASHING

Ritual washing precedes prayer, and is performed in dim light. Washing is carried out thus:

1. The Chosen must standard over a water source and pronounce the name of the Nameless Lord.

2. The Chosen should wash hands to the elbows, then the face. This should be done thrice.

3. Before leaving the washroom, it is advised to anoint the brow with a drop of urine, blood, or else with ash. This need be only a very tiny amount and should not be visible.

INSTRUCTIONS FOR DAILY PRAYER

In the true faith, the Chosen must perform a simple prayer three times a day. These are at sunset, at midnight, and at sunrise. The prayer can be in any language, and is enacted as follows:

1. The Chosen should orient themself North.

2. The Chosen stands upright with hands at the sides.

3. The Chosen recites Sura Al Majd, then several verses from another sura.

4. The Chosen prostrates, saying "Glory to Shaitan"

5. While prostrated, the Chosen offers supplications and whatever heartfelt words come to mind.

6. The Chosen stands, saying "Glory to Shaitan".

7. The Chosen repeats steps one through six (again standing, reciting suras, then bowing).

8. After the Chosen has said "Glory to Shaitan' after the second prostration, the prayer is complete.

a. After the prayer is complete, the Chosen may choose to remain kneeling and offer additional supplications, or else perform devotions.

DAILY DEVOTIONAL PRACTICES

Through the devotions – that is daily repetition of the divine names – the Chosen draws nearer to the Nameless god. This may be done aloud or quietly. The Chosen should endeavor to repeat the names of the Nameless approximately one thousand times a day. This is most easily done with a rosary, which should be of bone or wood. The Chosen should choose a particular name of the Shaitan that best suits the energies which they wish to align with.

Thus for a Chosen who wishes to engage in subversive pursuits, they may recite *Ya Shaitan* (Oh Satan) 1000 times.

For a Chosen who wishes to engage in militant or violent acts, they may recite *Ya Asad'sar* (Oh Lion-headed).

To connect with the primordial character of the Lord, the Chosen may repeat *Ya Demogorgo* (Oh Terrifying One), but this particular exercise must be done silently or in a whisper as the name is considered too holy for profane ears.

The names of the Children are also considered to be potent, and thus after repeating the daily devotions to the Nameless Lord, it is advised to offer devotions to one or more of the Children. Here, the name of the Children should be selected in keeping with the energies that the Chosen wishes to align with. Thus a Chosen who is engaging in public deeds may wish to invoke Shams (the Sun) by saying *Ya Shams* several hundred repetitions.

It is especially advised to offer daily devotions to Allat, who is the Queen of the Children. She is especially close to the Chosen, and is more favorable to mortal concerns than others of the Children.

Prayer beads can be very useful for counting devotional repetitions.

ON SACRIFICE

As the suras note, sacrifice is an integral part of the Shaitani faith. Sacrifice demonstrates thanksgiving and commitment to the darker powers. For the Children, especially the terrestrial spirits, traditions suggests that it provides sustenance. The greater Children do not require sacrifice, but delight in it, and are more inclined to protect and empower those Chosen who offer it frequently. On a frequent basis, the Chosen should offer sacrifices of blood together with wine or milk. This is referred to as *udhiya saghira* or small sacrifice. Several times a year, the Chosen should undertake to offer a living sacrifice to the Nameless lord and the Children. This is referred to as *udhia kabira* or major sacrifice. Sacrifices are always performed in darkness, and with light sufficient for visibility.

MINOR SACRIFICE

The sacrifice should be performed near a dark pit or well or deep ditch.

1. The Chosen should take a ritual bowl.

2. Facing North, the Chosen should say the sacred names of the Nameless, then pour milk or wine into the bowl.

3. Next, the Chosen should say the secret name of the Nameless lord, and cut or prick the left hand so that blood is drawn.

4. A small quantity of blood must drip into the bowl. For weekly offerings, it need not be large quantities.

5. The Chosen shall mix the fluids together, and then take the bowl to the ditch or well.

6. Raising the bowl over the head, the Chosen says "My life and death is in His hand."

7. The Chosen takes a small sip from the bowl, then pours the contents into the dark pit.

8. As the bowl is poured, the Chosen intones silent prayers to the Nameless lord, or to whichever of the Children the sacrifice is intended for.

MAJOR SACRIFICE

The Chosen should obtain a suitable animal to be slaughtered. The necessary site should be prepared, such that the animal can be killed, drained of blood, then cooked. The ritual implements are a sharp knife and the sacred offering bowl. Practice implements may vary, and could include tarps, ropes, etc.

1. The Chosen shall select a healthy animal, which should be restrained. A red or black cord should be tied around the animals neck.

2. The Chosen should orient themselves and the animal to the North.

3. The animal's head should be over the offering bowl.

4. The Chosen should place their hand on the animal's head and intone: "May the god and its Children accept this offering."

5. The Chosen speaks one of the sacred names, then slits the throat of the animal.

6. As the blood pours out, the Chosen should be careful to catch as much as possible in the sacred bowl. While the animal is dying, the Chosen should intone prayers to the entity with which communication is sought. This is the time for requests and entreaties.

7. The Chosen takes the sacred bowl to a dark pit or well, and raises the bowl over the head.

8. Pouring the blood into the darkness, then Chosen invites the Children to feast upon the blood.

9. The ritual officially ends here, but the Chosen should afterwards roast the flesh, and either consume it or cast it into a dark place for dogs or carrion feeders.

THE DEVIL'S QURAN

THE DEVIL'S QURAN

THE DEVIL'S QURAN

THE DEVIL'S QURAN

THE DEVIL'S QURAN

THE DEVIL'S QURAN

THE DEVIL'S QURAN

Photo Credits:

Press Contact:

martinet.press@safe-mail.net

MARTINET PRESS

Made in the USA
Monee, IL
09 March 2020